Resonant Recital

Resonant Recital

Devika Basu

Hawakal Publishers

Published by Hawakal Publishers, 185, Kali Temple
Road, Nimta, Calcutta 700049, India
Website: www.hawakal.com

Contact: info@hawakal.com

First edition (paperback): December, 2018

Printed and bound at *S. P. Communications,*

Kolkata

Cover designed by Bitan Chakraborty
Cover art: Canava

ISBN-13: 978-93-87883-46-8

Price: INR 250/- [USD 7.99]

Dedicated to my beloved mother, Hasi Basu.

Introduction

Let me confess at the outset that I do not write poetry. Strange it might seem, but when I go through the lines I have scribbled, I find myself in a strange paradox. The real and the imaginary often merge, and I find those lines nothing but an honest confession. The paradigm of poetry appears to lose its way to enter the tidbits of my life with 'me' as an omniscient narrator. I don't even know how the multiple domestic spaces have silently crept into the poetic zone. However, I cannot avoid accepting this bitter-sweet truth. It's up to the readers to decide whether these lines can be read as poems or an 'apology for poetry.'

Devika Basu
December 16, 2018
Uttarpara, Hooghly

BEREAVED BANQUET

My friends lit the light
on my 25th birthday.
Silver jubilee marked
with jubilant faces.
The *salwar* suit was red,
fragrance felt.

Forties bring birthdays,
pastries served,
gifts numberless.
Hands missing to bless.
Forties come,
in a bereaved banquet.

I have seen him suffer
bed-bound, his limbs tried
to meet the world though.
He bade me goodbye
on my first visit
to the sea.
He breathed the tumult
in my eyes.
Moonlit rocks touched
his wet bed-sheet.

I smelt the salt.

I feel the fragrance
when my father
used to count banknotes,
neatly built, tens and more.
I smashed them
once, twice, thrice…

My father smiled,
Oh dear, are you crazy?
Now it's my turn.

I find banknotes funny,
fresh and fine.
Uncut diamonds, locked in
bankers' paradise.
Fragrance lives in fragments.

In my childhood
I used to drink
cardamom tea.
My father showed red eyes.
I gave a mischievous smile.
He said,
Don't make yourself
a slave.

Now in my early forties
Pavlov haunts me
at 6. 30 sharp.
I see my father's face vaporized.
I am a slave,
slain to morning tea;
my father was right.

He won't come again
to chant his verses
at sundown.

In the wee hours
he won't sit in the balcony
in biting cold,

his hands are frozen
the quilt neatly built.
He sleeps there,
ready to sing
the hymn of death.

My youth has gone
to a distant land.

Spring shed its leaves
in the dusk.
My eyes have grown
in the dark.
Nights spent in my father's bedchamber.

He could feel the touch.
His vibrant eyeballs spelt
the syllable of death.
My desires grew with time,
father reclined on the backrest.

BROKEN WALLS

In my first date I asked,
Do you know what is love?

He smiled mischievously.
A four letter word
or lunatic spell .
Love is divine, elders say.
In my Masters I had read
'amor vincit omnia'—
love conquers all.
Glorious goal indeed!
A four letter word,
when we first met.

I adore him, I will.
His silver lining has a real punch.
Enviable moustache to carry loads of love
even in seventies.
My puberty touched his hands
moist, neatly built.
I grew up with time;
limbs, fragile.
I never saw him again.
Yet I hear the church-bell-ring.

I still love that smell
the walls, reminiscences.
I can feel the crippled bed-sheet.
My rosy lips in your bosom.
I can see antique frame of
your mother's photograph.
Her eyeballs, vibrant.

I still smell the scent in your
tired bed-lamps.

So far yet so near to me
like the first tender rays
of the rising sun.
Quivering lips stoop to kiss
the blessed dream.
Dreams are real at times.
Near me, tangible.

The real fades away.

On my first break up I felt the sting...
My breasts are dry,
lips frozen in withering cold.
I needed time for nourishment.

When I stand in the balcony
I gently watch the honeycomb.
'*Ripeness is all.*'
Night, memories and oblivion
all in a row...
Wedding night too short to sustain
memoirs.

My counselor looked at me over her specs.
She read my face, half done with compact pink.

Fifty is just a number, I must say.

She hurled me back to my childhood days
of geometric shapes.
Red eyes hidden under pilfering desk.
I stood in the dark,
my teacher waved kisses in blue.

Waitress came.
Eyeballs rolled in silhouette stain.

DISJOINTED FRAMES

Words come to me as disjointed frames
in solitary darkness.
Touch embedded in my pen.
Who am I to write?

I leave my desk and gently pause.
My pen tells the tamarind tale
in blue.

Sometimes words come to a halt.
A fragile tool to express numbness.
Solitude marks...

Windows rattle to catch moments
of unspoken raindrops.
My pen gets drenched in seasonal showers.
Words gush out in silver strain.

I fail to scribble moments in verse.
My days are spent in graphs countless.
I breathe in sleeping pills.
What if I am finished?

My words will remain in domestic archive.
My hands are tied and syllables numb.
Poems or nights written in rhyme?

It's not I who write
but 'self' confined in rain.
Words hidden in spring
gush out like birds,
liberated from sailor's cage.

It's not I who write.
Numbness reaches the zenith.

SEASONAL TEARS

Seasonal tears wash away our sorrows
in silence. Decaying leaves feel the magic touch.

Rain pours in like unending climax.
Griefs vaporize.

Dawn-kissed clouds gather.
The sky, enveloped in a holy darkness
stares at me in pure surprise.
Ethereal it seems to walk with the morning dew.

Flashes of light in the dark spread their wings
to rhyme with the divine.
The journey begins.

This monsoon I am lucky to have *hilsa*.
Dinner dishes welcome rain.
Temptation and fall story,
four pieces suffice.

I feel the smell,
frying pan personified.
My maternal uncle smiling,
fresh burns...
Hilsa in my veins.
Childhood caresses washed in monsoon rain.

MIDNIGHT MEMORIES

Last night I woke up to a dream.
Foam in the sea trying to catch
time in myriad forms.
My limbs drenched in waves, numberless.
Hands outstretched…

A quest, infinite and me.
Dream touching the Timeless.

Night beacons at me
in crystal silence.
My eyes are full,

hungry Mediterranean
looks at me
from the depths
of numerous waves.
I look back,

waves unfurled
in deadly despair.

Let me wade through darkness.
Night walks in benign grace
let me speak to the hungry tide
that engulfs me, my solitary self.
Raindrops permeate my eyes
in a canopy of darkness.
The leaves breathe with me
I tremble, leaves too.
Let darkness walk with me

in a divine crepuscule.

Night peeps in
blessed dreams usher
in pillows neatly built.
Midnight memories merge
with the earth's lullaby,
nightmare comes like
a featherless bird
touching the hollows of darkness.
The earth wakes up
her quivering lips betray
wounds of unrequited love.

Night peeps in, with dreams.

Memories converge at night,
corridors run to catch
time in a row.
History speaks through
silent walls,
night brings memories.

Blessed moments glide by
floating lights illuminate
our drooping souls.
Nights build a pleasure dome
in verse,
frenzied faces recuperate
from nightmarish thoughts.
Images float in rhyme,
moments glide by.

If you look at night
with a watchman's eyes
the street lights will
greet you in benevolence.
Traffic will pause to think
how busy is the road
in glaring lights.
Night is solitude
you are free to walk in silence.

Solace seeks me
in a splash of rain.
Rare moments flow,
orchids bloom
in autumn's balcony.
It's me and my soul
awakened from deep
slumber.
Solace seeks me
in autumnal bliss.

A dreamer I am
in the grey hours of solitude.
I watch the ebb of Time
a chameleon moves
with changing colors.
Dreams too have their names.
Innocent wishes grow
in the womb of time.
Dreams sprout
in adolescent nights.

In grey hairs though
I still cherish to grow.

Weary nights cross
the balcony of silence
when I am alone.
The Witches come
to greet the night
with venomous wombs.

The sky turns red,
I gently walk,
my careful steps
cross the threshold
in benign silence.

My cup is full
'fair is foul' I know.
Night stares at me
in sheer dismay.
The enchantress comes
in clairvoyant castles.

Dreams knock at my door
at crimson night.
Moments set out
in silent ecstasy,
my limbs run
to catch time.

A celestial cry
is heard
from the depths
of the sea.
Dreams come true
I believe,
in flickering light.

ETHEREAL

No, I am not going to brood.
The moon has its crevices
it fades away with time.
'Now' is the word to live
and no looking back
to our doted dejection.

The river is full
to pour in moments
rhymes and mirth.
Every octave holds to its name
until it finds a concluding couplet.

I have been lunatic
since childhood.
'Poet, lover and lunatic'
haven't been crammed
into my brain
till then.

Wilson made it all
I feel while
I dote on
moonlit *Faraglioni*.

My first crush
was the moon
I might say.
The moon is pale now,
so am I
with crevices due.

I SMELT THE SALT

The rolling waves
split time into fragments.
The morning sea or
serenity personified
loneliness reaching the zenith
to penetrate,
decaying love plays
an autumnal tune.
Todays look back
into yesterday's dreams
in flashing meadows.

The seashore stands alone.

The waves washed my feet
at night.
Rains replenished my eyes
I walked along the beach.
Memories hid their faces
in veiled clouds,
a splash drenched me.
The rain-soaked memories
drenched in April shower.

Take me to the sea
I will touch
the sand-washed waves.
Midnight melodies merge
in sonorous sea.
Let me chant
the hymn of silence
amidst countless waves.
The seashore calls
to feel the crimson hue
in forgotten dunes.

MY WALLET IS TOO FULL

My wallet is too full
to contain despair.
The coins grow with time
my tired eyelids
fail to count
banknotes, fresh
from the mint.

My deepest longings
hide their faces
in wallet walls.
Miseries, wallet, coins
wait in the lounge,
ready for the
next flight.

Of late I have felt
smoke in the air
denizens of darkness
permeate my soul.
Crevices, wounds and death
entwined in filial bond.
A little voice, arms outstretched
enthralled in bewitching silence.

Her eyes are grey
lips unable to speak
she uttered, at last
fragments or poetry
steeped in pain?

No, not now
she is sleeping
let her sleep.
Her hands are tied
she bleeds
let her grow in grief.

One blow will strike
a discordant note
in her sleep.
Let the waves roll
in utter dismay,
let blood spill over
the dismal silence.

Let justice wake.

The sun has set
horizon turns red
memories rain
in lonely graveyard.

We breathe, our
poems await
resonant recital.

Incense steeped in blue
tolls the knell of death,
forgotten words hide
beneath a veiled perfume.
Death levels all
moribund corpses lie
in the crowded burning *ghat*.

Pious priests chant
the final prayer of life
the pyre waits in flames.

Incense burns, desires in ashes.

Let's retreat
our walking shadows
seek recluse in sand
our hands smeared in blood
limbs frozen.
Their faces are dry
loins groan.

Give me light to watch
smoke in the sand
I have seen gluttony's face
rattling in the window seat
of my delayed flight.
Let me touch you
in the decaying lights
of autumn's cubicle.
Enough is felt
in this deadly paradise.
I have read
The Seven Deadly Sins
at midnight.
I feel tired now,
let me watch the night.

THE THIRD EYE

Krishna walks barefoot
the field is dry
Garlands wait
to greet life

The wheels move
Krishna looks back
in utter surprise
Karna in the field, alive!
His piercing eyes
ready to defy
Divine betrayal

Krishna stands still
The wheel stares at Him
A scavenger's look
to face the real battle.

The third eye it was
To behold evening's decadent note
My sixth sense, active as ever
Seemed to tell me
a tale of vengeance.
How did he feel then?
Lord said, "Look straight and make
it right now."

The broken wheels seemed to tell
the unspoken agony of history.
Third eye was it, piercing into
the bloody, as they say,
"Blood will have blood."
Now I stand, history behind
Asking desperately,
"You too Brutus?"

Make the guns ready
shoot to the core
keep them at gunpoint
muffled voices speak
the truth unheard.
Evil, like an epidemic
prevails over good
solemn silence in the air;
guns ready to bid adieu.

Silence in the womb.

Acknowledgements

I'm grateful to my teacher, Dr. Kuntal Chattopadhyay, who has been with this collection since its inception. He has gone through my poems diligently, and his suggestions have certainly added to the anthology.

I am indebted to my friend, Sonali Datta, who has inspired me to enter the arena of creative writing.

My sincerest thanks to my dear students, who have always been a refreshing presence.